Two C
of Edinburgh Folk

FLASHBACKS NO. 1

The Flashback series is sponsored by the
European Ethnological Research Centre,
c/o the National Museums of Scotland,
Queen Street, Edinburgh EH2 1JD.

General Editor: Alexander Fenton

TWO GENERATIONS
of
EDINBURGH FOLK

Dorothy Slee

CANONGATE ACADEMIC
in association with
The European Ethnological Research Centre and
The National Museums of Scotland, Edinburgh

First published in Great Britain in 1993
by Canongate Academic
an imprint of Canongate Press
14 Frederick Street Edinburgh EH2 2HB

© Dorothy Slee 1993
Published with the support of the Russell Trust

ISBN 1 898410 04 6

Cataloguing-in-publication Data:
A catalogue record for this book is available
on request from the British Library

Typeset by Hewer Text
Printed by Cromwell Press, Melksham, Wilts

Contents

Foreword

This first volume in the *Flashback* Series has been written by a former member of the National Museums of Scotland's staff. She came to me one day and asked for a project, in order, as she put it, to prevent her brain from seizing up as a result of a heavy dose of administrative duties. I proposed that she should begin at home, assembling recollections from her mother, and adding her own to them. She did so, adding selections from the photographic record also as she went along. The result is the present volume on *Two Generations of Edinburgh Folk*.

I am grateful to Dorothy Slee for having carried out her homework so well and expeditiously. In addition, the exercise produced the spark that has led to the concept of the *Flashback* Series, in line with published collections on the stories of individuals that have appeared in other countries, such as Norway. The term 'Flashback' was, in fact, her inspiration, so that in completing the first volume of recollections, she has laid a groundwork for much else.

The *Flashback* Series is an exercise in oral history. Every single individual, every family has a story to tell. Everyone can add a quota to the total sum of knowledge of human history. The Series presents snapshots of the lives of individuals, in their positions in space and time, and as far as possible in their own words. As it grows, it will contribute increasingly to knowledge of local and personal history, which can then be set alongside the work of political and other kinds of historians.

Anyone who wishes to help should write to The European Ethnological Research Centre to ask for a copy of the *Flashback* Guide, available free. It can be used by individuals, or by groups.

Reference numbers in the plate section refer to negatives in the Scottish Ethnological Archive, National Museums of Scotland.

Alexander Fenton

Introduction

An entry in the 1861 Census return for Buckhaven, in the parish of Wemyss in Fife, begins the story:

John Logie	39	fisherman
Janet	44	
Grace ⎫ Barbara ⎬	10	
Walter	8	
David	6	
Janet	4	
Johanna	2	

The number of rooms with 1 or more windows – 2

At this date the youngest child of this family, Isabelle, was yet to be born. Johanna was my grandmother, her daughter, Gracie, my mother. The two generations of recollections set down here are those of my mother and myself. They cover over half a century of Edinburgh life.

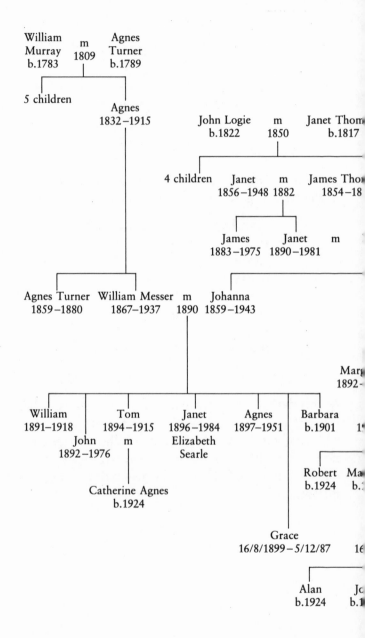

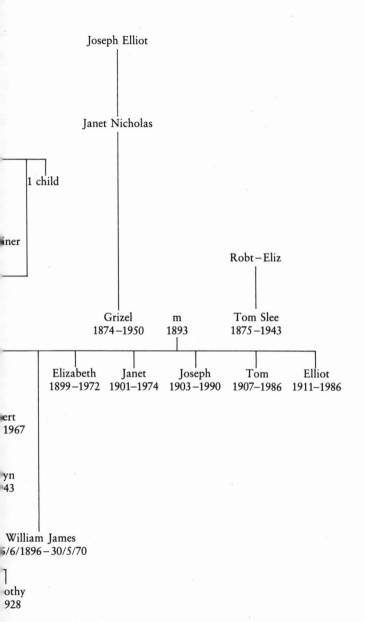

Joseph Elliot

Janet Nicholas

1 child

...iner

Robt – Eliz

Grizel   m   Tom Slee
1874–1950   1893   1875–1943

Elizabeth   Janet   Joseph   Tom   Elliot
1899–1972   1901–1974 1903–1990   1907–1986   1911–1986

...ert
1967

...yn
...43

William James
...6/1896 – 30/5/70

...othy
928

Part 1

Gracie

Johanna was born on 8 January 1859. She recalled her upbringing as strict, with an emphasis on religion and temperance, typical of the small fishing communities huddled along the Fife coast. In later life she rarely spoke of her mother, but she had clearly been strongly influenced by her father and his elder sister, Aunt Kirsten (Christian). The children played a lot on the beaches of Buckhaven. They were still of golden sand as the pits had not yet thrown out their mountains of black waste.

On the Sabbath, a day to be respected, the children's time was spent either at church or at home, reading the Bible or learning the catechism or poetry from their mother. This poetry, which mostly had a religious overtone or a sentimental theme of a family in stress, was remembered for the rest of her life and recited at length to her children and grandchildren. Here are extracts from two of her favourites:

THE MARTYR CHILD

Randolphus, Lo, I bring to thee
The palm branch from on high,
For unto thee this day is given
For Jesus Christ to die.

The Prefect knew his parents well
And fain would save their child.
So now he speaks persuasively
In accents soft and mild.

"Randolph," he said, "thy fault ere now
I freely will forgive.
Offer some incense to the God,
Great Jupiter, and live."

*   *   *

They bind him to a pillar now.
They scourge the noble boy.
No sound of pain escapes his lips.
His heart is filled with joy.

*   *   *

Oh, radiant is Randolphus' face
And bright his upturned eye.
"I am a Christian and for Christ
Oh joyfully will die."

*   *   *

He bows his head, the sword descends.
His earthly course is run,
While angel hosts exulting cry,
"Martyr of Christ, well done."

May we, like thee, so live and die,
That when our course is run,
Jesus shall say to each of us,
"Soldier of Christ, Well done."

An orphan child was Jenny Lee
Her father, he was dead,
And very hard her mother worked
To get the children bread.

In winter time she often rose
Long ere the day was light
And left her orphan family
Till dark again at night.

And she would always say to Jane
Before she went away,
"Be sure to mind the little ones
and don't go out to play."

*   *   *

And when the babes were safe to bed
She neatly swept the hearth
And waited for her mother's step
Come sounding up the path.

Then open flew the cottage door,
Her weary mother smiled,
"Ah, Jenny dear, what would I do
Without my precious child."

Local employment in Buckhaven was either the fishing or the pits for boys and the net factory for girls. Mother must have decided against the latter, as she went into service in Edinburgh as a nanny.

The records in New Register House contain a certificate of entry of illegitimate birth of William

Messer Murray, born at Dirleton in East Lothian to Agnes Murray, washerwoman, on 8 September 1867. He was the second illegitimate child of Agnes Murray; she had borne a daughter in 1859 who was to die in childbirth at twenty-one years of age. In such circumstances, early life must have been one of poverty and hardship for these youngsters. William was apprenticed as a baker, and by 1890 was working in Edinburgh, where he married Johanna Logie on 16 September 1890. He was twenty-three and she was thirty-one. Father never talked much of his childhood except to recall seeing a horse and cart disappear in the soft sand at Aberlady Bay. Their family was soon established:

William	born	28 June 1891
John Logie		23 September 1892
Thomas McMinn		19 June 1894
Janet Thomson		9 July 1896
Agnes Turner		21 December 1897
Grace Logie		16 August 1899
Barbara Logie		24 October 1901

There were all family names, except Tom, who was called after the postman! As was customary then, a family photograph was taken when the family appeared to be complete; plate 2 shows the Murray family in 1903.

Father was a kindly easy-going man who liked to socialise with his friends of an evening in the local pub. His opportunities for such camaraderie were limited, however, as mother carried the responsibility for the family's slender budget and all household affairs, and there was little money to spare for such pleasures. She possessed the stronger character of the two, bringing up the family much as she had been brought up herself, though not so strictly. Our home was happy and secure with the constant voice of mother humming or singing hymns as she busied herself about the house.

In the early days there was no question of buying a house. There were plenty to rent and the family moved about in the village of Stockbridge (Stockaree) as the family grew—and grew up. We lived at different times in four houses:

1890–1893 19 Henderson Row, a two-roomed flat
1893–1897   5 Hugh Miller Place, a three-roomed lower house in the Colonies
1897–1911 20 Hugh Miller Place, a five-roomed upper house in the Colonies with an external stair.
1911– 76 Hamilton Place, a six-roomed top flat tenement house which was eventually bought in 1926.

I lived at 20 Hugh Miller Place and at Hamilton Place until I was married in 1923. The house at number 20 had three rooms downstairs and two above, one of which was grandma's residence from which she rarely moved. She was a little woman with a humpy back. As children we thought the hump was the result of a slip on a banana skin, but it was more likely due to years of bending over the wash tub, which was how she earned a living. Grandma, my father's mother, had her own furniture and ornaments, like the pair of dainty little brass candlesticks which we were allowed to play with, and the goffering irons for the mutch she wore in bed. Her mutch was a close-fitting linen cap with frills at the edge which were crimped into place with the goffering iron, similar to the old-fashioned curling tongs. Grandma must have done some cooking in her room, as I was sometimes sent to buy a halfpenny worth of vegetables for soup. In the other upstairs room slept the four girls—all in one bed with two heads at top and at bottom; we seemed to take it in good part when the odd foot was thrust in the face. In the winter the beds would be warmed with stone pigs, those heavy earthenware hot water bottles with a protruding stone stopper in the middle. There was a kist in our bedroom for our clothes but I remember only one wardrobe in the house. Our furniture was sparse but practical, and always second-hand. The acquisition of a chiffonier, a display cabinet, for the parlour was a source of great excitement; this came from Lyon and Turnbull's saleroom, where our neighbour worked. The kitchen had a press in one corner and boasted a long whitewood dresser with wooden slats underneath, where the family shoes were stored. There was a white deal table, scrubbed daily, and plain wooden chairs. There were not enough of these to seat all the family together so I often had to sit on the fender with Barbara to wait our turn at table.

Cooking was done on the range—the coal fire with two hobs on swivels, an oven at one side and a boiler with a tap at the other. It was my weekly job to blacklead the grate and 'emery' the fender, a task which was carried out in a most desultory fashion. The blacklead polish was applied to the black parts of the range with a special brush which had a hoop handle the length of its spine, and then vigorously polished up with a bit of old velvet rag to achieve a shine. The steel parts and the fender were burnished with emery cloth, an abrasive mineral on a cloth backing. Lighting was provided by a noisy gas light with a glass globe, which 'plopped' incessantly.

Father worked as a baker, 5 a.m. to 5 p.m., with W.K. Bain at Warriston Bridge, now a Chinese restaurant, for 21s a week. By afternoon he would be out delivering bread in the Inverleith area and we would be sent along to collect a few loaves in our basket. When Bain retired, father took over the business and Nettie and I worked in the front shop for a while, but neither he, nor we, had much of a head for business so that little profit was made. Bread was 3.¼d a loaf and morning rolls, including delivery, were seven for 3d— and the good folk of Inverleith expected a discount on a weekly bill of 1s 6d for their rolls. There were some lighter moments. Father made water biscuits, but not the others like rich tea, digestive or creams. When a traveller called on one occasion, I gave an order and, in response to his 'Water?', I advised proudly, 'We make our own water'. Midst embarrassed smiles, Nettie commented that that was a bit of a *faux pas*, to which the sharp traveller responded—'More of a fu' po'.

Our provisions had to be bought from the 'Store'—otherwise the Co-op—on account of the dividend of 4s 4d in the pound which was a marvellous nest-egg to help out with the rent money, the finding of which was mother's eternal problem. Our share number is imprinted in my memory—26797. But no matter how short money was, father would always manage a halfpenny each week to each of us for pocket money.

The Colonies of Stockbridge are a series of cul-de-sacs so arranged that each street consists only of upstairs houses or ground-floor houses. When we lived at 20 Hugh Miller Place all the houses were accessed by an external stair, one side of the street being Hugh Miller Place and the other side Rintoul Place; the low doors of Hugh Miller were opposite the low doors of Reid Terrace, the next street. Each of these little streets formed a separate community of families. We lived and played with the Coopers, the Mallens, the Nicholsons, whose father worked in Lyon and Turnbull's saleroom, and the Ross's, whose father worked in Clapperton's, later to become Maule's, then Binns and finally Fraser's at the West End of Princes Street; Lottie Ross was to become my friend for life. She was a proper tomboy and harum-scarum, who taught me that bells were for ringing and then running away. There was little traffic in these days and the Colonies were a safe place for children to play.

I cannot remember mother in other than mainly black often glinting with embroidered beads; she would sometimes wear a blouse with a little white in it, and she would wear a white cotton apron with a bib front, or a waist-high crash (coarse linen) pinny while she was working about the house. As youngsters, our clothes, at least our warm winter clothes, were either passed down or second-hand; only my eldest sister, Nettie, might be lucky enough to get a new dress to wear beneath the cotton pinnies that we all wore. I recall feeling a little ashamed at being taken to Mrs Pritchard's second-hand clothes shop in St Stephen's Street with mother. In the summer mother would make us all spotted muslin dresses beneath which we wore a petticoat and a cotton chemise gathered on a tape. Everyday footwear consisted of leather buttoned boots over black stockings, and in the summer, either bare feet or rubbers. Our clothes were always well patched and mended.

For special days or parties we would don black patent ankle-strap shoes and a specially made party dress. Our hair was worn long, held back by ribbons, until the age of about fifteen when it was 'put up'. When it came near bedtime we were called up from play in strict age order, to have our hair small-tooth combed, then brushed and put up in rag rolls. The boys wore Norfolk jackets with Eton collars and breeches over long socks. Canonmills and Stockbridge Public Schools provided all our education, except for Nettie who went for a time to Broughton Higher Grade School. In Stockbridge we had four teachers – one from age five to seven, another from seven to eleven and a third eleven to fourteen, plus a sewing teacher, in my day the dreaded Miss Davidson. We would close each Friday with the song 'God be with you till we meet again'. My school days are hazy, but I know my favourite subjects were mental arithmetic, parsing and grammar, one of which I must have performed sufficiently well to merit an end-of-term prize. But the glory of this achievement was lost when my idealistic teacher, Billy Renton, displayed his scorn when I chose *Troublesome Ursula* rather than *John Halifax, Gentleman* for my prize. At other times I would get strapped for talking in class, but not before being fortified by Lottie's friendly nudge and whispered advice 'Dinna greet, Gracie, dinna greet'.

We were sent off to school with a handful of raisins for the break, after a breakfast of porridge and bread with jam. Our food was plain but wholesome and we were never hungry. Dinner at one o'clock was the main meal. Soup would be broth, real thick stuff with leeks, peas, carrots, turnips and barley, or leek and rice soup with flank of mutton for stock. We were given a lot of stovies for dinner and sometimes pease brose. We would not have meat every day but we often had a kipper or potted herring, or mince or stewed rabbit. Puddings were custard, semolina or curds and whey, made with rennet; all would almost certainly be accompanied by the interminable –

P R U N E spells prune, eating them is your doom
Life's too hard—death comes too soon
To fill our tummys with the darned old prune!!

I recall tea as simply tea and either toast or bread spread with jam, sugar, dripping or treacle. From the end of his knife Willie could draw the finest pocket watches with his treacle.

At Easter we did not have chocolate eggs, but we did roll hard-boiled eggs. We would wrap the egg in lots of layers of onion peelings in a rag bound with thread and boil for about 20 minutes. The finished article provided a multitude of pictures for a child's imagination.

The special food for Christmas seemed only to be the home-made plum pudding boiled for hours on the fire. There would be trinkets for all. Santa Claus came in by the chimney or, more likely, the lum, so the stockings were hung there. It was with great anticipation that we crept down early in the morning to claim our stockings and excitedly feel the contents—at the toe, a whole penny, then an apple and a mandarin orange, some sweets and some small toys, a wooden doll and a colouring book perhaps. We did have one large doll and a doll's teaset which was shared among the four girls. At Christmas there was usually a visit to the pantomime at the Grand Theatre nearby. Birthdays were remembered when it would be a practical present from mother—gloves, stockings or the like. As well as buying sweets with our pocket money—and a halfpenny went quite a long way then—we would buy some liquorice root to make a 'sugarollie' drink by soaking the root in water and giving it a daily shake until it was ready—I think, well coloured.

Our ailments, which were few, were treated with castor oil, sulphur and treacle or Epicacuana wine, a herbal tonic for coughs and colds. I always had chilblains in the winter and had Zambuk ointment applied.

There was no bathroom in the house, just a toilet, and when it was bath night, a round wooden bath tub was dragged in front of the kitchen fire. The laundry was wheeled in an old pram to the wash-house in

St Mary's Street, off Raeburn Place, until the Co-op introduced the bag-wash; this was collected from the house and returned fairly damp to be dried on the kitchen pulley. Mother would do the ironing on the table which was covered with a blanket; the iron, the solid cast-iron sort, would be up-ended at the fire to heat and deftly wiped on a cloth before use.

Holidays for the boys meant the Boys' Brigade camp, while the girls were packed off to Auntie Janet in Buckhaven on the *Red Gauntlet*, which sailed from Granton to Methil. Mother's sister had been widowed when she was quite young and left to bring up our two cousins, James and Janet. Auntie Janet earned a living from a little general store at the corner of the street and augmented this income by taking in mangling for a farthing a pin. In the old box mangles, the heavy wooden rollers round which the clothes were wrapped were called 'pins'; a pin of laundry was as much as could be mangled at one time. It must have been at no little inconvenience that she squeezed into her tiny house four extra girls each summer to relieve the pressure on mother. I used to sleep on the kist at the foot of James's bed. As regular visitors, we got to know all the local children, some of whom were our cousins from other branches of mother's family. Most of our time was spent roaming the beaches and rocks gathering wilks for boiling or 'helping' Auntie Janet catch the partans; and there was always the excitement of mother's visit to look forward to.

Sundays always had a special aura about them, unlike today. In the morning, I, always the soft mark, was sent downstairs to get the bibles so that we could sing hymns in bed; at the same time I would collect the special Sunday treat that mother left on the kitchen table—usually a bag of boiled sweets. After breakfast we went to the children's service in the church hall in Dean Street, and when we were older, to the church with father in the morning, but it was always Sunday School in the afternoon followed by a walk in the park or gardens; no play was allowed. When I was quite young mother had given up the church after being deeply offended by the minister, Dr Fiddes, when he had called at our house to see grandma and did not spare the time to chat with mother. She did not, however, give up her strong religious faith. She turned instead to the Salvation Army, which she supported for the rest of her life. To please her, I accompanied her once to one of the meetings and I can recall the inner trembling as I crept forward to the 'penitents form' to confess my sins.

As far as our church connection was concerned, the highlight of the year was the annual Sunday School trip. This was anticipated with great excitement long before the big day. We would be turned out with gleaming new tinnies, tin mugs, tied across our chests with new white tape, usually new rubbers and often a bunch of cherries pinned to our crisp white pinnies. There would be races, games and, of course, the bag of buns. Part of the thrill was the fact that we travelled by train—to such places as Arniston, New Hailes or Spylaw Park. Otherwise, much of our entertainment was of our own making, mostly street games. On the outside stairs the girls would be playing 'schools' while the boys would demonstrate their oral expertise as 'ministers' by playing at 'churches' in the cellar under the stair. There were singing games, skipping ropes, diabolo and the ever popular peevers (hop scotch). The best peever was undoubtedly a slice of marble, but this was rarely available so the usual tool was a flat boot polish tin or a Zambuk tin. Oh! the horror when a half-full tin of Zambuk, taken without permission, disappeared down a siver (drain)! The boys played more with peeries (tops) and guiders, a home-made contraption on four wheels steered with a bit of rope, or gave the girls wheelbarrow rides, and progressed to bikes when they were older. In the summer, we would all walk to Granton for a picnic or play in Inverleith Park. We were banned from going near the Water of Leith, which was close by.

We normally only played with the children in our own street, but the exception was on Victoria Day, 24 May, which was bonfire night. Then we joined forces with youngsters from adjacent streets to collect for our fire. The Colonies always had two fires, one at each end of the rows of streets, and there was great competition between the two ends for the biggest fire.

St Patrick's Day on 17 March was another day specially marked, and this was a sort of perpetuation of the Irish problem. We armed ourselves with balls of newspaper bound with string with about two feet left for a handle. We then challenged each other 'Scots or Irish?'—if Irish, they would be whacked on the head with the paper ball.

By the time I was ten or eleven, Lottie would induce me to go up to Princes Street for a free cable-car ride. A penny ha'penny transfer ticket allowed the passenger to ride on the cars, at snail's pace, from Stockbridge up to Frederick Street, then change to another car to the top of the Mound. Lottie had learned that a number of people did not take the second half of this journey, and it was among the discarded tickets at the Mound that we searched for the unused stubs to afford us the free rides.

In her spare time mother would be reading the *People's Friend*, or latching a rug with rags or wool, while father spent a lot of time over his daily paper. He supported the Hearts football team along with the boys, while summer evenings were reserved for the bowling green at Inverleith or his allotment at Warriston. Some evenings mother and father would have friends in for a game of cards—a game called 'Catch the ten'.

We all left school when we reached fourteen to earn our own livings. By today's standards we were a large family, and because of the difference in our ages, I was closer to my sisters than the boys. Willie worked in a shop at first, then went into service at Cleghorn in Lanarkshire and later as foot-man at Saltoun Hall, near Pencaitland. Throughout his life, Willie corresponded regularly and it is clear from these letters, many of which were kept, that he took very seriously his responsibilities as eldest son and support for mother. The following letter from Cleghorn, sent as a fifteen-year-old, provides an account of his first reactions to life below stairs:

1st June 07

Cleghorn House
Cleghorn
Lanark

Dear Mother,

I received your parcel all right and I am very pleased with the contents as the ties are the very same as I wished them. I have been waiting at the table this last two or three nights and I am doing all right. I have got a tail coat and a red vest for waiting with and another suit for going out in the carraige. I bought a tie for myself which cost 5d but I think you should get them cheaper in Edinburgh. Everything is so very dear out here. I also bought writing paper and Envelopes and some stamps which I am now using. I set the Servants dinner table every day and also the supper table. Tell Tom that I get plenty meat out here. I get all sort of fruit and the best of meat. I think that Tom's teeth shall be wattering when he heres it. I am very pleased to get a shirt to change as I thought I would have to keep on my old one for another two Months as we get payed Quarterly starting on 15th August and so on most of which I will send home. Tell Nettie and Aggie that I cannot promise them any present untill I get some pay as I have not a penny to Bless myself. This is a fine country place as it is all woods and fields. I was going for a walk yesterday afternoon in the woods by the side of the narrow river when I saw a number of rabbits run out of a hole. I gave chase and got excited and picked up a stone and threw it but I think that I missed it. There are a great number of Rabbits and Grouse in the grounds which the gardeners are trying to get rid off as they come into the fields and spoil the crop. I am at great friends with all the gardeners and Woodmen and often have a talk with them. The old Butler hase been 50 years in the house and hase now reached the age of 76 years he is Retiring on September first as he is to old to work. I have not written to John William yet as I am very busy but I will write about the middle of the week and tell him how I am getting on. I suppose he will be surprised not to see me in Edinburgh on Sunday. I am always thinking of what is going on at home as I am very weary but will soon get accustomed with it I suppose.

Tell Mrs Nicholson that I thank her very much for the pair of Scissors that she gave me and the knife as they come in very handy. I will be 16 years of age on the 28th of this Month but I don't expect any present this year as you have not got the Money X ha', ha', ha'. The trains pass through the grounds on their road going to Glasgow and I sometimes don't get sleep for them. We get a Fort nights holiday when we are about a year in the house so I will come home then if possible. It has been very wet weather this last two or three days and I have not been able to get out for a walk in the afternoon. I have that Black Suit of Clothes which I do not need so I will send it home when I get money and it will do for John or Tom for wearing at the School. As I think it would not be fit for wearing when I Come home. We also have prayers every morning in the Library room where Mr Lochart reads a Chapter out of the Bible and also says a Prayer which we always repeat. I also answer the door and take in the Party's luggace and Place it in their room and take all the things out and put them into the Drawer or the Chest. I have had no signs of making any tips yet so I am beginning to get Down hearted. I clean the boots in the Morning first thing and then get the Breakfast table ready. I have got a fine easy time of it here. I am doing nothing all forenoon and nothing all afternoon. It is very quite out here this is not like a Saturday in Edinburgh no football matches or Games. There is some Sports coming on Shortly called the Lanimers in which all the old Lanark people dress up and Make a procession through the town in carts it is very comic I suppose. The old Butler was telling me about an incident which happened at the Lanimers last year. An old man was fighting with another man in a cart with Rabbits (dead ones of course) and drinking bottles upon bottles of whiskey at times collapsed in the cart and fell dead in among the Rabbits and all the people laughed instead of being sorry. (This was the cause of drink.) We are very busy just now as their is Company in the house (4) Ladies and (1) Gentelman and they are all English and never been in Scotland before. I expect a little tip from them when they go away on Monday. I got a nasty cut with a piece of glass—between the finger and the Thumb and There is no signs of it healing up. Sometimes I have to go out and gather Black and Red berrys as the Cook makes her own Jam. I have to wear a Round hat on the Sundays to go to the

Church with. And a Tile hat like a coachman's for going on the carriage. My Finger was so sore this morning that I could hardly wash my face. Mrs Lochart was telling me that I should Stick in and She should get me a Job as a footman alone and I am just going to do so and please the old man as best I can. When we Arrived on Tuesday at Cleghorn the old Butler was at the door of the Carriage to let Mrs Lockart out and when he saw me he said to Mrs Lockart that is a decent lad he is strong and tall and will get on better than the last one if he behaves himself. I will be at church tomorrow with the rest as we all go to the same church (the Established) except one English Servant who goes to the Episcopol Church. I have never had a bad word said to me yet although the old Butler often gets Excited but I never mind him so I get on. Mrs or Mr Lochart never stop in my work the old Butler does the Boss. I was not feeling very well yesterday I think that it was my finger that caused the sick feeling to come over me, but I am all right now. I hope you are all well at home. My fingers are getting sore with writing so I close my letter giving love from Willie to all of them. I shall have to get up to wait dinner as it is 8 o'clock. "Saying"

> Good Night
> Your loving Son
>
> (Sgd) William

During the next few years Willie tried various sorts of work, without finding his particular niche. In this·

period he took to camping and cycling holidays in England and Scotland with his close friends, Douglas Fairbairn and Willie Dewar, 'The Terrible Three', as they were known. In 1911, at the age of twenty, he joined the army as Gunner in the Royal Field Artillery and at last he found a challenging and satisfying occupation. John and Tom must have been impressed with his reports of army life and the smart uniform, as they both very shortly followed suit. Thus when I was still an eleven-year-old, the boys had all left home.

Willie was posted to India early in 1913. There he matured and successfully rose through the ranks to the Officers' Mess. As well as providing an account of his life in India, his letters reveal the changes that took place in his character, ambitions and general outlook on life and the strong affinity that existed between mother and him. But he was destined never to return to Scotland for which he became so homesick. He was accidentally killed in Baghdad on 30 July 1918, so near the end of hostilities. His last letter home, written two days before the accident, was carried by mother in her handbag until her death in 1943.

John enlisted in the Scots Guards, rising to the rank of sergeant; he distinguished himself for bravery in the field and was awarded the Distinguished Conduct Medal. He married in 1917 and, after the war, emigrated to Western Australia under a scheme specially devised to open up the bush for agriculture, a most arduous task. Although producing prize-winning crops, there was no market for them and the scheme collapsed. John, Lizzie and the daughter they now had, Cathie, returned to Edinburgh a bit disillusioned after seven years of hard work with little to show for it. They settled in Hamilton Place for a few years until they got their own home. John became a well-known face in Edinburgh as he finished his working life as doorman at the General Post Office helping all and sundry with their queries. John lived to the age of eighty-four.

Tom was the harum-scarum in the family, well known for being a sleepy-head. He enlisted in the Royal Scots Fusiliers at the age of seventeen and a half years. His army career was to be shortlived. He was sent to France and was killed in action at Neuve Chapelle when he was just twenty. His body was never identified as a comrade had taken his disc and the contents of his pockets to return to mother; he was therefore reported as 'missing, believed killed' for some months until eventually deemed to be killed in action. When this final notification was shown to Auntie Janet from Buckhaven, she immediately recognised his number—6320. Some months previously she had been kept awake all night by the continuous recurrence of this number. We all got new black clothes purchased from Lawson's in Lothian Road and paid-up weekly.

During our early years the social life of the four Murray sisters was derived from the various clubs and organisations of St Bernard's Parish Church, Girls Guildry, Lifeboys, tennis club and the Girls Association, the 'GA'. As each started work making new friends and developing new interests, we gradually parted from these activities, but all of us continued association with that church for life.

My two older sisters, Nettie and Nan, never married, living on in the family house at Hamilton Place until their deaths, Nan, prematurely at the age of fifty-three and Nettie at eighty-eight. Nettie started work in the local post office where she became adept at tapping out telegrams in morse code. She spent some time as shop assistant in a gents' tailors shop and in father's shop, after which she worked for many years in J.W. Mackie Bros., rising to shop manageress. For the final twenty years of her working life she was a clerkess in the office of William Younger's Brewery, an occupation that was never divulged to mother who would not have approved because of her strong temperance beliefs. Nan spent all her life in the publishing business, first in the Edinburgh Press, then with T. and A. Constable.

My first job was in McLagan and Cumming in Warriston Road where I stirred a glue pot for five shillings a week, so I didn't stay there for long, but moved to the fruit department in the Civil Service store in George Street where my pay increased to nine shillings. I then managed to get a position in J.C. Smith, Tailors, in Lothian Road at a weekly wage of fifteen shillings. The business was owned and had been built up by Joseph Carnachan Smith, known as the 'Guv'nor' to all the staff. He was a strict disciplinarian but liked and respected by the staff. His imposing figure complete in morning suit was always at the door in the mornings when you arrived, early or late! He directed all the business himself, and if there was doubt about making a sale we had to 'fetch the Guv'nor'. Business was brisk after the war when the demobilised soldiers flocked to buy grey flannel trousers and tweed sports jackets. After I had left to be married, the Guv'nor died and was succeeded by his uninterested son who allowed the firm to decline and eventually go into liquidation.

Barbara and I both married in 1923—to two brothers.

Part II

Dorothy

Grace was married in 1923 and I was her third and youngest child, born in 1928.

I can just remember my grandpa, her father, who died in 1937 when I was eight years old. He had silvery white hair to match his clay pipe. I would be told to 'Wheesht' while he tinkered with his 'cat's whisker' or crystal wireless set, tuning it for a decipherable sound. Grandpa had an allotment at Warriston which we would visit to get fresh pea-pods, and we would sometimes go to Inverleith Park to watch him on the bowling green.

I knew my granny much better as she lived with us for about three years before her death in 1943. She had white hair held back in a bun at the nape of her neck, twinkling grey eyes, an erect carriage and seemed to me to have a tranquil and contented disposition. She was a bit deaf and we always had to remember to speak up clearly to her. Granny kept my sister and me well supplied with cosy hand-knitted ankle socks; we would sit on a sunny doorstep in the Spring with new yellow socks and new leather sandals feeling very well clad indeed. Granny spent a lot of time sitting at the front-room window, and would announce to the family that (say) '235 people have passed along East London Street this afternoon'. Her poems, learned as a child, were her great party pieces delivered in a strong quivering voice, which often sent us children into fits of giggles—and trouble. Granny always took it upon herself to wash the tea dishes and was so avid about this chore that saucers and plates would be whisked off to the sink as the cup was raised to our lips for the last sip. Thereafter, she would sit with drumming fingers in anticipation of a game of rummy or bezique, or the time to go off to her Salvation Army meeting. On a fine afternoon her outing would be for a seat and a blether in Gayfield Square gardens which was a meeting place for many of the old folk in the district.

My Dad was William James Slee, second son of the eight children of Grace and Tom Slee of Kielder Station in Northumberland, where grandpa was a railway surfaceman. Kielder grandpa, as he was known to us, was born at Kirkby Stephen in Cumbria and later moved to Longtown where he met granny, a direct descendant of Robert Elliot, the Gretna Green parson. Grandpa was a small man with a bushy moustache—he used a special moustache cup for his tea—and he was canny, soft spoken and very kindly to his grandchildren. In contrast, granny was tall with a rather throaty voice, kind in her own slightly gruff way, and she was the grandest of bakers; her scones, ginger cake and apple cake were a real treat. She was almost always enshrouded in a floral apron, topped with a battered old black felt hat, not only when she took us to feed the hens, but, also, quite often, in the house too.

Dorothy

The little station house, adjoining that of the station master, was exciting for us town children, as it was so different from our own home. It was quite small on ground level with only the porch, one room and the larder, which was under the stairs. This, the living room, was also the den of Winkie, their bad-tempered tom cat. Cooking was done on a traditional blackleaded grate which had a swinging arm for the kettle, and above were two cupboards flush with the wall. The ceiling had wooden beams with hooks in them from which there might be a side of bacon hanging, if a pig had been killed recently. Upstairs the house extended over the station waiting-room and contained three bedrooms. I remember gazing in awe at the large jugs and bowls in each, the collector's items of today. There was no toilet in the house; there was only the one in the station waiting-room. The water supply was located outside at the front of the house where there was a tank and a tap, just at the roadside. Water was carried from there to the bedrooms and to the porch where the household washing was done. My Dad, or Bones, to give him his pet name, worked on farms around Kielder as a lad before coming to Edinburgh about 1919 to work with the LNER railway. Here he met mother and they married on 16 July 1923. They had three children—

Alan	born 9 July 1924
Joan Margaret	born 10 August 1926
Dorothy	born 11 September 1928

What planning and organisation did it take, I wonder,

to have exactly two years, one month and one day between each of us!

Being a railwayman, Bones was subject to shifts starting or finishing at any time of the day or night, and we had therefore to live within a reasonable walking distance of St Margaret's goods depot at Piershill which was his base. When they were married, my parents rented a three-apartment second flat in Brunswick Road, and this was where I spent my first five and a half years. My recollections of the house are scant except for the swing that Bones had suspended from two hooks in the doorway between the kitchen and a bedroom. The house was in a narrow street overlooked at the front by houses while the back faced onto a concrete drying green, beyond which was a suburban railway line.

In 1935 we moved to Cochran Terrace, a small cul-de-sac, to a flat with an additional room and a closet large enough to accommodate a double bed. The house was bought for £350 of which a large proportion was borrowed at an interest rate of 3.5% per annum. It was a big step to take on a mortgage with a growing family, but Mum's fears about the wisdom of this move soon vanished when it turned out that the mortgage payments were amounting to no more than costs of renting. We moved in on a fine day in May. I cycled along on my trike and Joan pushed her doll's pram, but not before the minor drama of the Pickfords' van not turning up and Mum having to seek an alternative contractor. Bones was at work, leaving one house and returning to another; time off meant no pay. Being on the second flat, the house was light and bright with larger rooms and an open aspect on both sides. Our neighbours were Mr and Mrs Farquharson, with the Bruces and Williamsons above and Docherty and another Bruce below, while on the ground floor lived the Knights and the Watts. It was an asset that all these families were amiable and friendly. Mrs Farquharson, who was to become a firm friend of Mum's, must have been apprehensive about the new neighbours, so when she enquired of the previous owner what the new folk were like, she was told—'They are very nice; Mrs Slee wears good gloves'. These would be one of Mum's sales bargains from R.W. Forsyth's! The house was re-wired for electricity—there were previously only electric lights and no power points—and the very latest Triplex grate was installed in the kitchen. This provided two ovens and it had a back boiler for hot water. Our cooking was done on the fire and on an electric ring which stood on the raised hob which ran the length of the grate. Gone forever were the days of blackleading.

This house was farther from Bones' work but still within walking distance. Bones was a steam train man, first as a fireman and, later, a driver. Most of his working life was spent on goods trains, but towards the end of his career he was obliged to change to diesel passenger trains when St Margaret's goods yard was closed. His shifts were most variable and were arranged in series called 'links', through which the men moved with seniority, the more senior links containing the more acceptable shifts. Work on the steam trains was quite hard—both firing the engine and handling the heavy levers—and the pay in those days was poor. In the early 1930s Bones was earning a basic pay of between £8 and £10 a fortnight, and his highest basic pay at the end of his working life in 1961 did not exceed £13 a week. His daily lunch, at whatever time, was a bottle of tea to be heated up on the engine, and sandwiches with perhaps an apple or a piece of cake. His piece tin would sometimes be brought home full of gowans collected at some signal halt. Very often one of the first things he did on reaching home was to bathe his eyes, as eyefuls of cinders were an occupational hazard. Time was important in the old railways and Bones had to file a report if his train was late—even by a minute. When he was put onto a new route he would write out his timetable on a scrap of paper, to be kept handy in his waistcoat pocket. For such chores he would use one of the tiny pencil ends—just an inch long—he stored in his pockets. Bones never just took up his pencil and applied it to the paper. As a golfer may perform a few practice swings, Bones' pencil would gyrate above the surface of the paper before the writing actually started.

There was no such thing as sick pay in those days. All pay stopped on sick absence, but there was a payment of fifteen shillings per week from the Rechabites of which he was a member. The Rechabites is a Friendly Insurance Society for total abstainers, the members of which can get financial assistance when in special need. Great hardship resulted, therefore, when Bones was hospitalised twice for surgery, first in 1930 for a mastoid operation, and again in 1937 for kidney stones. It was on the latter occasion that the special treat of a picnic was replaced by the calamity of my losing a purse with 19s 8d change in it. Mum told me later that Kielder granny helped out financially at this time, and about then Mum used to take in a few paying boarders.

But her most lucrative bit of entrepreneurship, generated by need, was in the early 1940s, when Alan had started at the Royal Dick Veterinary College and I suppose Joan and I were costing more to clothe. That was when she went into business as a maker of soft toys, albeit in a small way. The raw material, fur fabric, was scarce in wartime, so a lot of second-hand stuff was used and the odour of damp disinfected cloth hanging on the kitchen pulley is still vivid. After some trial and error a range of toys was produced—teddies, Scottie dogs and terriers, rabbits and golliwogs. The enterprise became a family operation with Bones handling the technical details, such as making sticks for packing and fixing discs and rivets so the teddies' arms and legs would swivel, and Alan, Joan and I stuffing the toys and doing some finishing-off work. We earned something like one shilling for stuffing one article and sixpence for doing a golly's hair, eyes and 'grass' skirt. But undoubtedly the weight of the project fell on Mum, for as well as all the sewing, she had to hawk suitcases of toys round retailers until a regular group of stockists was established. When the war was over and the shops were again filled with furry toys, our little business, which had served its purpose, just faded away.

The old treadle sewing machine was a vital piece of equipment in our house. All the remnants Mum picked up at the sales were made into our clothes. She would tackle anything—coats, skirts, kilts, dresses and blouses. The scraps of woollen material were always set aside, and when a bagful was collected, Joan or I would be sent up to Nathan's rag store in the Cowgate with the instruction to say 'tailor's clippings'; the bag would be weighed and we would take home a shilling or two.

Daily Life

Our main meal was at midday. I remember leek and potato soup because I didn't care for it, and Mum's superb apple dumpling because I adored it. Tea time was about five o'clock. This was high tea, something savoury followed by bread, tea-bread or cake. I was once offered the choice of 'half a kipper or a *whole* banana'—a bit of psychology applied when kippers were in short supply. This was not a grand meal and we filled up with bread spread with jam, syrup or treacle. We must have had voracious appetites as I recall that when visitors were present, we were always reminded to 'FHB'—Family Hold Back—lest we polished off all the special goodies leaving little for the poor guests. There was no such thing as sliced bread then. We would buy either a plain loaf, a square pan or a french or high pan loaf, all different shapes, which would be wrapped for us in sheets of camel-coloured tissue paper. We were always told to ask for a 'cutting' loaf, which was the previous day's baking and a copper or two cheaper. I would sometimes be sent up to Rose Street Lane where Mackie Bros., the bakers in Princes Street, had a cut-price shop for selling off the

1. John and Janet Logie. *SEA: 51/50/14.*

2. The Murray family, 1903. Grace, front row, 2nd left. *SEA: 51/49/5.*

3. Grace Murray at Father's shop. *SEA: 51/49/3.*

4. Father (left) at the bowling green. *SEA 51/51/9.*

5. Kielder Granny and Grandpa. *SEA: 51/51/3.*

6. Granny and Grandpa. *SEA: 51/50/10.*

7. The Kielder Slees before Elliot was born. Dad, back row right. *SEA: 51/50/13.*

8. Mum and Dad, 16 July 1923. *SEA: 51/50/11.*

9. Dorothy, Alan and Joan, 1936. *c 18449.*

10. Largo: Granny with Cathie, Alan, Joan and Dorothy. *SEA: 51/51/10.*

11. Mum and Bones, 1963.

12. Alan, Joan and Dorothy, 1990.

previous day's produce; a favourite from there was a rough wholemeal loaf called a 'CP', though I never knew what these letters stood for.

Bones liked to try his hand in the kitchen too and he was no mean cook when it came to puddings. He could make the finest rice and raisin pudding I have ever tasted and he would always break an egg on the top before it was finished off in the oven. He would also make a barley or macaroni pudding in the same way, which I think was something he got at home as a child. There was usually fruit in our house—oranges, apples and bananas—a case of apples, forty pounds, cost twelve shillings in the 1930s.

At Christmas Kielder granny would send up a parcel of her home baking and some home-made butter, much to Bones' delight. Christmas also meant roast chicken and a plum pudding with the chance of getting a silver threepence. The plum duff had been made weeks before with each of us having a lucky stir at the mixture before it was boiled. Coffee was almost unknown in our house even at Christmas, but then there would be sherry or port for the adults and ginger wine for the children. Bones had signed the 'pledge' as a lad and he never, in all his life, drank any spirits; cider was his favourite beverage.

We hung up our stockings at the fireplace and left a glass of milk and a piece of cake on the kitchen table for Santa Claus. When with excitement and anticipation we awoke while it was still dark, we would hesitate about rushing to the kitchen for fear the stickings were still limp and empty. But we were never disappointed. The filled stockings always contained an apple, a silver-wrapped mandarin orange, a sixpenny piece and some chocolate coins along with sundry small gifts such as crayons, scraps or transfers, and one main present—perhaps a doll, a manicure set or a toy shop. But what I best recall playing with were Alan's things—his Hornby train set, Meccano, gyroscope or that wonderful wooden ark complete with Noah and two of each animal. We spent the morning playing with all our new acquisitions and after lunch would set off for Granny's at Hamilton Place for tea. There we had more presents and games and always the Christmas tree with lights.

Birthdays meant gifts, special food and sometimes a party; Bones' birthday on 26 June heralded the first strawberry feast of the year. His presents were limited to baccy or a new pipe; St Bruno or Erinmore flake, and the pipe was preferably a City de Luxe with a cherrywood bowl.

Hallowe'en was also a party occasion—dooking for apples, treacly stones hanging on swaying strings which had to be eaten with hands clasped at your back, hunting for nuts secretly hidden in the parlour and, lastly, in the apple tub, half walnut shells with slices of lit candle in them. The last candle to extinguish got the prize. Before the dooking we always joined hands in a circle and sang this verse:

> Hallowe'en is here, once every year.
> Apples rosy red, floating water clear.
> Stand upon a chair, hold your fork in air,
> Drop it now, you've got a big one!

School was something I took for granted; I neither

liked it nor disliked it. We all went to the local primary school and Alan progressed to George Heriot's while Joan and I went to Broughton Secondary School. For five years there I enjoyed the hockey pitch, the tennis courts and the maths lessons. The rest I merely put up with. I found out-of-school activities much more interesting.

On the domestic side we would be given chores around the house, dusting, tidying the bedroom— ugh—or the favourite of polishing the floor which was more of a game as we tied dusters on our feet and skated about to achieve a high shine. We would all take our turn of running messages. In Broughton Street there was Mr Brooks, the butcher, Coats, the chemist, and Knights for potted meat. Mr Knight had a grey parrot in a cage at his door, which was always a diversion. At the corner of East London Street was Mr Cormack's grocer's shop where more often than not you would be met with the fine aroma of freshly ground coffee beans—not that I ever purchased such luxury, though on special occasions Bones sometimes made coffee in a pan. When the war came along it was with Mr Cormack that we were registered for all our provisions. The wall behind the counter was lined with wooden drawers of varying sizes, each provided with a scoop to ladle out the contents—lentils, barley, peas etc.—into stiff brown bags, the tops of which were then expertly folded and tied with string.

Mum taught Joan and me the mastery of the treadle sewing machine, first on paper without thread until we could sew a straight line, and we were introduced to cooking and baking guided by a Bero cook book;

a well-scrubbed hand is still the best tool for blending the fat and sugar for cakes.

Of an evening there was the Band of Hope or the Brownies or Girl Guides, or we would go to a mission group held outside at the foot of Little King Street, now obliterated by the St James Centre; this was well worth a visit as, instead of having to take a penny for the collection, we were given a penny for attending! There was sometimes a free picture show at the Deaf and Dumb centre in Albany Street where Felix the Cat featured—'Felix kept on walking, kept on walking still'. We also visited the commercial cinema—mostly the Ritz in Rodney Street where we could get in before four o'clock on a Saturday for twopence. Joan went to tap dancing at Mrs Luscombe's Dancing Academy in Windsor Street; best remembered is her 'Shoe Shine Boy' when Mum made her a black sateen evening suit for the annual concert.

If Bones was off duty at weekends we would go on an outing to the King's Park to feed the ducks or to climb up the slopes to St Margaret's Chapel, to Leith docks or along Granton breakwater. Sometimes we had a sail on the *William Muir* from Granton. There would be annual visits to the zoo when we got sixpence for broken biscuits to feed the animals. We would rummage in our bags to see who could first jubilantly produce a whole biscuit. I seem to recall that we had the lion's share! A favourite for Bones on a Sunday evening was the Mound where I got to accompany him when I was older. There were the political and religious speakers, some with large bands of supporters and others with few, like

Charlie, the bean man, so-called because he constantly chewed chocolate lentils—now called smarties. Our two aunts would also take us out: to tea at the Sealscraig at Queensferry or to Harwell's at Colinton after a visit to Colinton Dell and Spylaw, or up to the shops in Princes Street with Auntie Nan, while Auntie Nettie preferred to take us on a picnic to Dirleton or to Crichton or Borthwick Castles, and sometimes to the woods at Queensferry from the ferry at Cramond.

An exciting event each spring was the Royal Infirmary Pageant. We would help to raise funds by donning fancy dress and selling flags on the Saturday morning. We set off in pairs to scour the streets, one with the tray of flags and the other rattling the can. Cathie once brought me home in tears after I had tripped and ruined all my flags on a wet pavement—but the flags went into a slow oven and we were soon sent out to finish the job.

Sundays started with a 'surprise'—a bar of chocolate or some sweets left on the kitchen table—a practice started by granny with her family. Sundays were best clothes, Sunday School and Hammy (Hamilton Place) for tea. Best clothes included a black velour hat complete with school badge at the front in the winter, and a white panama in the summer, and Sunday School was at St Bernard's Church in Stockbridge, which was the family church. If we set off early we had time to play a few games en route—car number spotting, or counting the many 'For Sale' and 'To Let' signs on the houses, and we would be able to see the boys from Fettes College complete with shiny black toppers and striped pants filing into St Stephen's

Church, but we often seemed to be running at the last minute and would arrive huffing and puffing with a stitch in our sides.

Hamilton Place for Sunday tea endured for many years. In the 1930s Uncle John, Auntie Lizzie and Cathie lived there as well as Granny, Grandpa and the two aunts. It was a large gathering and the tea table wasn't big enough to seat us all in comfort, so the four children were placed at their own little table in a corner. This arrangement had advantage and disadvantage; we could lark about and not bother too much about table manners but we didn't have access to the full range of cakes, a big attraction at Hammy. Aunt Nettie worked in J.W. Mackie Bros., the bakers in Princes Street, where the staff had the chance of a "3d bag", a bag of surplus cakes sold off on Saturday evenings—rum babas, meringues, cream baskets and pineapple cakes. After tea there was a set of Children's Encyclopedias to explore, or the chance of a hurl on a woolly rug across the vast expanse of the lobby lino. In the parlour was the tigerskin rug complete with head, plus bullet hole, and a stuffed snake, both of which had been sent back from India after Uncle Willie was killed in 1918. Other novelties included the piano, the little harp and the gramophone with its large trumpet and winding handle, though it was funniest when it was running out of puff. The closet off the hall was our gang hut where the four of us had our secret feasts of carrots and sugary water, the basic ingredients for which Cathie had 'saved' throughout the week. There we used our gang names, Alligator, Cats, Jumbo and Dog. Auntie Nettie and Uncle John must have walked us home sometimes as I can yet recall the strained neck as the Plough, Orion, the planets and other heavenly bodies were pointed out to us.

While we went visiting on Sundays, the family came to our house on weekdays. Saturdays often saw Uncle John and Auntie Lizzie for a game of cards, when fish and chips were the order of the day, and Auntie Nettie and Auntie Nan visited us on Wednesdays and Thursdays respectively. Auntie Nettie usually read to us in bed and we were introduced to 'Prossie' in the *Tale of Two Cities*, the *Count of Monte Cristo*, and other shorter tales which she reeled off. On our own, we filled our heads with the usual childish rubbish— *Dandy, Beano, Film Fun, Wizard, Rover, Hotspur, Champion* and the *Girls Crystal*. The only stalwart now remembered is Wilson, the great all-round athlete. Granny took the *People's Friend* and was keen on Annie S. Swan, and I seem to see Mum with *Titbits* and *Answers*; Bones confined himself to the evening paper and the *People* on Sundays where he liked to read Hannen Swaffer's column.

We had regular visits from our relatives in Buckhaven, especially Auntie Janet, pronounced 'Jennet', who was Mum's cousin, and her husband, Uncle Dave. Until she died in 1948 at the age of ninety-two, Auntie Janet's mother, who was granny's sister, would often accompany them for the jaunt. Grandma Janet, as we called her, was a small woman with penetrating blue eyes and smooth rosy cheeks though the rest of her face seemed to me to be very wrinkled. She was a most calm and contented person. Grandma Janet was never without her knitting, which was always grey socks, and even when she was a very old lady, her stitches were firm and even. Auntie Janet's favourite handwork was crochet with fine cotton. Her cheval sets, runners and tablecloths still abound in the house. Uncle Dave was a great gardener, so that their visits always brought a bouquet of flowers and a load of fresh vegetables. On these visits we all had to remember to wait at table before eating until Uncle Dave said the grace. There would be prods and nudges below the table if it appeared that any of us was forgetting to wait, and suppressed giggles if Uncle Dave invited Bones to say grace.

Bones' relatives also visited us but these visits were rarer as we saw most of these relations during our holidays at Kielder. But Lottie Ross, Mum's old friend from childhood, paid an annual visit when she was in Edinburgh with her family. Lottie will always be linked, for me, with Ferguson's Edinburgh Rock, a poke of which she brought for each of us from Ferguson's shop in George IV Bridge. Lottie and Mum were friends for life. When they were together they always ended up happily recalling their childhood in Stockbridge.

There were a few characters to be seen about town in those days—the little old lady with the trembling hands who played gramophone records outside the Playhouse, the bearded violinist in Frederick Street, the lady with a monkey and a barrel organ drawn by a pony who could usually be found round about the West End, the hot peas and whelk seller in the Lawnmarket. Newhaven fisherwives adorned in their striped aprons and shawls used to sell fish round the doors, and 'Ingin Johnnies' in black tammies were a familiar sight on their bikes laden with ropes of neatly strung onions. There were ragmen happy to swap balloons for old clothes and wailing back-green singers to whom Mum would throw a coin wrapped in a bit of newspaper.

We didn't ail much. There was the whooping cough which sent us off to the sea air at Largo, and Joan and Alan took scarlet fever and ended up in the City Hospital. All three of us took the measles at the same time. I remember lying in bed with the blinds drawn, Mum walking round the room with a hot shovel of steaming carbolic to disinfect it.

Holidays and Play

Holidays were Kielder at Easter or summer and Largo in our early years. Largo started when we all had whooping cough and the doctor suggested a change of air. Granny rented a cottage at Largo for us for a month and it was such a success that we returned there annually for six or seven years. The little rented cottages were at the far end of the village of Lower Largo, just across a narrow road from the beach. Happy and carefree, we spent most of our time on this beach—building sand castles, paddling, looking for crabs in the rocks, or floating in a large rubber inner tube. There was the year when Alan had a raft made of wooden planks lashed to some oil drums with a long pole as a punt, and we soon learned that we had to watch the tides to avoid being swept out to the middle of the Forth. I well remember Alan having to lie flat on the raft with his arms fully extended into the sea to push us back to safe water. At the other end of the village by the Crusoe Hotel there would be pierrots and a Punch and Judy show to visit, where we would stand enraptured by the strains of 'Oh, Oh, Antonio' or 'Why am I always the bridesmaid never the blushing bride?'. We often had visiting relatives, especially Auntie Janet from Buckhaven, but we had to be sure not to let her see us at the Pierrots as she was a strict Baptist to whom such shows were taboo. We would sometimes climb up Largo Law and always have a picnic at Shell Bay which meant a trek along the beach laden with all the picnic gear and, most important, Grandpa hugging the large yellow melon.

When we grew out of Largo, it was always Kielder for holidays, where we would stay with Auntie Barbara and Uncle Bob at the 'Birches'. This was Mum's sister who had married Bones' brother. Our two cousins, Bobbie and Marjorie, were our companions. At that time Kielder was a mere clutch of houses round the station, though the 'Birches' was about half a mile up the road from the station. We always travelled by train as Bones could get either a free pass or a privilege ticket for us.

We came to be very familiar with the journey from Edinburgh, anticipation and excitement mounting as we passed Galashiels, Melrose, Newtown St Boswells, Hawick, Stobs Camp, Shankend, Riccarton Junction, where we would change trains, then Deadwater where the English border was crossed, and, at last, Kielder with Granny and Grandpa on the platform to welcome us. We used to look forward to that journey for weeks, and in so doing Joan and I would write each other letters which would be clearly labelled 'To be opened at Melrose' or some other station en route. I think the letters contained each other's plans for the holiday, just adding fuel to an already brightly burning fire.

Kielder had, and still has, a special fresh fragrance, perhaps from the pine trees, which was very noticeable to those coming from the town. It also had hazards for me: leaping over drains and ditches, watching out for adders and the impossible job of avoiding the accursed and abundant midges and clegs, which had a very strong desire to taste my blood. I bear their scars to this day. Life at the 'Birches' was very different from home. In those days there was no electricity and lighting was by Aladdin lamps with candles in the bedrooms. The wireless worked on an accumulator and was used sparingly. Uncle Bob was adept at switching it on exactly on the stroke of one or six for the news. Although fresh milk was delivered daily and Auntie Barbara had to scald the cans each morning, 'Ideal' milk is still Kielder to me. There was then no water supply to the house and all the drinking water had to be carried from a well at the roadside some fifty yards away and down a slope. We used the rain barrel water for washing. The dry toilet was at the foot of the large yard at the back of the house. Today all these circumstances would be regarded as privations but we took them for granted as just part of Kielder. It was a novelty for us to help carry up the water.

The house itself was created originally by Uncle

Bob from a First World War army hut—re-roofed, covered with white asbestos sheet and partitioned into rooms inside. Uncle Bob changed the shape of the house quite often.

As a lad Bobbie showed us how to make bows and arrows and whistles from the willow trees; he also impressed us with his skill at catching moles, whose skins he would dry and stretch, then possibly sell them, I think. While Bobbie could climb any of the trees like a monkey, Margy, Joan and I limited our climbing activities to the 'Bent' tree, an amiable nearby birch that had suffered an accident as a sapling, so that its trunk sloped up at an angle of forty-five degrees before reaching up to the sun. We knew every finger, hand and foot hold on it and devised five or six different 'swings'. The Bent still lives, but she now looks like a frail old lady. The threat of fire from the trains was present each spring, and if we were down at Easter we would take up post on the railway banking armed with a beater and hopeful of earning a copper or two from the Forestry for extinguishing a potential forest fire. Sometimes we did. While playing on the banking, we would get a wave from the driver of 'Wandering Willie', then sprint up onto the rails to collect the halfpenny we had placed there, now hopefully pressed out to penny size! We also visited Kielder Granny and Grandpa as well as Bones' brothers and sisters and their families, many of whom had settled nearby.

There were no shops at Kielder but we had no problem in spending our pocket money as there was a carrier nearly every day—Mason, Adamson, Jock the Store or Andy Fletcher—and there could be a Saturday trip to Hawick or Hexham. The Kielder of those days has now gone forever. Today there is a fine big reservoir and pleasure area, instead of the small farms where Bones worked as a lad. The new village has been built, along with a new 'M1'. The trains have long since gone with the Beeching cuts, and the castle, once a country seat of the Duke of Northumberland, has become a Forestry Museum. Alas, progress!

Play at home was in very different surroundings. Being a cul-de-sac, our street was a natural and safe play area and Bellevue School playground nearby proved excellent for bikes and roller skates. Apart from gazing in the window of Mrs Thomson's sweetie shop at the street corner and playing guessing games with the initials of the sweets in the rows of jars or playing between the red Brooke Bond tea vans whose depot was in the street, we would play 'kick the can', statues, peevers, skipping ropes, football, french cricket, diabolo or roam the district in a well organised game of 'leevoy'. 'Leevoy' was a team game with any equal number on each side. One side hid in the stairs of surrounding streets, Bellevue School playground and suchlike. After allowing about five minutes, the other team set out in search and, as soon as a member of the opposing team was spotted, he had to join the 'searching' team until that side had taken in all the other team. The name is an abbreviation of 'relieve-o', which is the name for the game in Northern English dialects.

There was a fair number of children in the sur-rounding streets, so you could be sure of getting someone to play with. We occasionally got into trouble with neighbours with stray balls. There was a nice expanse of wall between the windows of the flats next to ours useful for ball bouncing, much to the chagrin of the residents, since our aim was not too good. We competed to throw the highest ball and inevitably some hit windows or were doused on the roof (i.e. stuck in a gutter). In retrieving them Alan once succumbed to the temptation of popping a few down some of the chimneys—and they were sooty in those days! This brought the police to the door. Bicycles became the vogue when you reached fourteen or fifteen years and Edinburgh could be explored on two wheels, enjoying the freedom of roads with few cars, but with the hazard of tram rails to contend with: a bike wheel fitted very nicely into the tram lines.

Indoors there were our toys to play with or competitive family games of bagatelle, darts or table tennis, the latter on the kitchen table, fully extended. It sagged a bit in the middle and the balls bounced awry if they struck the join of the leaves but this only added to our enjoyment.

I was nine years old when Mum took us to the Empire Exhibition at Bellahouston Park in Glasgow. Auntie Nettie was with J.W. Mackie Bros. at the time and she was working in their shop at the exhibition which, of course, we visited. The Mounties in the Canadian Pavilion, the thatched cottages in the Clachan and the folk art in Africa House impressed me almost as much as handling my first telephone in the Post Office Hall. There was a laughing sailor in perpetual movement at the Fun City. While I timidly enjoyed the crazy mirrors, I was very frightened just watching the big dipper, which Mum seemed to adore. I seem to recall that one way of leaving the Fun City was by sliding down the Helter Skelter on a mat. In fear of being separated from the rest of the family, I eventually rode down after much cajoling in apprehension and terror. Eating out was a novelty for us and it was at the exhibition that I experienced my first self-service restaurant. I never thought of having to pay at the other end of the line so I took everything I fancied. It must have been a highly embarrassed Mum who made me put most of my load back on display.

War

The declaration of war in 1939 brought us up with a jerk and filled us with a sense of impending doom. This came from Mum who had lost two brothers in the last war. Alan's secondary education was not to be disturbed but Joan and I were to be shipped to the safety of Canada and had already received all the embarkation papers, when an evacuee ship was torpedoed in the Atlantic and the scheme was abandoned. Instead we were evacuated from Edinburgh under the local authority arrangements with our school. In the first week of September we were assembled in the playground of London Street School and given milk and bananas plus a carrier bag containing, as far as I can recall, a packet of digestive biscuits and tins of syrup, condensed sweetened milk and corned beef. Mum, sporting an armband to show she was a *bona fide* voluntary helper, accompanied us, though her motive was, no doubt, simply to see us settled safely. Eventually we were transported to the Waverley Station and put on a train—destination unknown! As well as school children, the evacuation catered for mothers with babies and toddlers. All were packed into the carriages, rife with rumours as to our destination and filled with the noise of howling babies and the smell of wet nappies and regurgitated milk. At one point we pulled to a halt somewhere in Fife and the rumour spread—'It's Kingskettle, it's Kingskettle' – but eventually the journey ended at St Andrews. It was clear that the powers that be did not consider that Leuchars aerodrome would be a Nazi target, unless they had planned to get rid of us! We were lined up in the playground of the Burgh School where chaos ensued as the august citizens of St Andrews claimed their new boarders.

After the slow and frustrating journey it should be noted that we were not in the fresh, pristine condition in which we set off. I am sure the townsfolk were each seeking the cleanest looking children with no mothers in tow. Joan and I along with Irene and Billy Millar, neighbours and school classmates, were claimed by Mrs V.C. Dalmahoy, a sprightly lady with crisp white hair and the spark of vitality in her eyes. We were taken by car to her home, 'Rockview', at The Scores, a sizeable semi-detached stone house of twelve to fourteen rooms on four floors, with a large garden adjoining stables and garage buildings. The house was perched on the top of cliffs above the sea at the edge of the Step Rock pool at the West Sands.

In addition to Mrs Dalmahoy and us, the 'vackies', the household consisted of Jean, the cook, Mary, the maid, and 'Ninnie', who had been Mrs Dalmahoy's Nanny and had been given a home for life, and who was to see to our needs. The other member of the household was Mr Law, the gardener, but he only came to work there one or two days each week; that Christmas he was presented with a miniature *Dictionary of Gardening* from the four of us, costing sixpence in Woolworths.

The kitchen and the quarters occupied by Mary and Jean were in the basement, though this was ground level at the back of the house. On the ground floor was the large dining room, Mrs Dalmahoy's drawing-room, a pantry, a toilet and the smoke room which was re-allocated as our sitting-room, while upstairs were Ninnie's room and the bedrooms. There was also a bedroom in the attic, next to the apple loft, which we sometimes used. We were allowed to explore the garage and the stables which were used to store all manner of interesting odds and ends—old tackle, skis and the largest wooden sledge we had ever seen and which was later to carry all four of us whizzing down Jacob's Ladder in the winter snow.

Everyone went out of their way to make us welcome. For example, although the evacuation only took place on September 3 or 4, an iced cake was quickly made for my eleventh birthday on September 11 with little parcels from all. Meals were very strange at first as we had to get used to the enormous size of the dining-room table with its starched linen tablecloths – a change from oilcloth—and to selecting the correct cutlery from the vast array at each place. There was a long sideboard on one wall from which we could select our breakfast cereal from half a dozen varieties and on which Mary placed the hot breakfast food in silver salvers with lids. We each had our weekly butter ration on separate little coloured butter dishes at our places alongside a starched huck napkin—another novelty for us. I remember for lunch Jean's syrup sponge pudding with its accompanying jug of hot syrup. But we must have been messy little devils, as Mrs Dalmahoy soon introduced a penny reward for the one with the cleanest section of tablecloth each week. We had milk and biscuits in the Smoke Room at 7pm, and bed for me was at 7.30pm. It was then that we would sometimes catch a glimpse of Mrs Dalmahoy in her dinner gowns—for she dressed each evening even though she was dining alone—these were long velvet dresses, crimson, black or royal blue. I think it was Ninnie or Mary who saw us into bed.

I attended the Burgh Primary School and my schooling was undisturbed as I had my own teacher from Edinburgh, at least to start with. Joan went to Madras College with none of her own teachers. One of Mrs Dalmahoy's friends was a teacher at St Leonard's School in St Andrews and she would on occasion help Irene and Joan with the homework. We were allowed to ride Mrs Dalmahoy's bicycle, but only on The Scores, which was a quiet road. It was, therefore, to my great chagrin when the front brakes jammed and I flew over the handlebars in College Street, and ended up in real trouble. I was banned from an outing to Dundee and reported to Mum. We were visited regularly by the family who would always be invited for lunch and tea; but I fear these visits only served to heighten the homesickness that I certainly felt.

We joined the Girl Guides and Mrs Dalmahoy took us on occasion to the local cinema or to visit her relatives in the town. We took walks along the Lade Braes, to the West Sands or to explore caves in the cliffs below the house. On Sundays we might watch the University students parading in their crimson gowns along the harbour wall. The old castle was adjacent to the harbour. On one occasion Joan and I slipped through a fence there and made our way along to a sloping parapet to watch the breakers pounding on the rocks. There was nearly an accident when I skidded on some seagull's droppings. But Joan was to the rescue, hauling me tremblingly back to safety.

It didn't help matters that many of our friends had begun to trickle home early in 1940 when the expected bombing of Edinburgh had not materialised. Despite the exceptionally kind treatment we had received, the overall effect of the evacuation on me was a feeling of resentment at being plucked away from home and placed in a strange house in a strange town in a different stratum of society; during our time at St Andrews I developed into an awkward child, deliberately flouting the rules of the house.

We returned home in March 1940 to a very different Edinburgh. White lines had been painted at the edges of pavements, on all steps and around the sides of car bodies; ugly sandbags protected some of the more esteemed buildings. Black-out was fully operative and many of the iron railings about the town had been removed to help the war effort. Binoculars were appealed for to pass on to the Royal Navy. Old net curtains were stuck to our windows to prevent flying glass. Of course food rationing prevailed and we were obliged to register at specific shops for meat, tea, butter, cheese and eggs. Points coupons for the likes of dried fruit and biscuits could be used at any shop that had supplies, as could clothing coupons and sweetie coupons. I was able to qualify for extra clothing coupons as my height was in excess of 5 feet 3 inches.

It is now known to be the case that the nation enjoyed better health under the wartime food restrictions on account of reduced intake of fat and sugar; I believe the weekly ration of the fatty foods was—butter, 2oz; margarine, 4oz; cheese, 2oz. Bones and Granny both qualified for extra cheese, three quarters of a pound a week each; Bones on account of having to carry his lunch and Granny because she had diabetes. Of course Granny was debarred from a sugar ration. A lot of novel food and recipes emerged at this time: Prem and Spam were types of canned meat; Snoek, canned whalemeat, was introduced; Pom, which was dried potato, dried milk and dried egg appeared on the shelves; the use of soya flour, high in protein, was advocated. We used soya flour with almond essence to make cakes—marzipan potatoes, rolled in cinnamon. For a main course meal we would have curried butter beans with carrots or boiled macaroni bound with egg and fried as patties. Oranges were scarce and bananas disappeared for the duration of the War. We wore luminous buttons on our lapel and had to carry our gas mask at all times. There were regular gas-mask drills at school. ARP (air raid precaution) Wardens patrolled the streets and back-greens nightly and would blow their whistles and call 'chink' if any light escaped your blackout. One day Mum and I decided to go to the pictures—it was Roddy McDowall in 'My Friend Flicka'—and, as had become our normal practice, we would black-out the house before leaving. So we switched on the lights and made to close the shutters on a sunny western sky, when at the last minute Mum decided that we would not go into the parlour when we returned. Alas the room was so bright that we didn't notice the lights were still on. On our return we found the house door forced and feared that burglars had been at work. The warden had got the police to force entry to switch off the light which was illuminating the entire neighbourhood—we were fined a few pounds.

We were to become familiar with the warning sirens for air raids, the frightening wail of the 'alert' and the steady, comforting drone of the 'all clear', and we soon were able to recognise the high-pitched drone of Gerry planes. Stray planes had a go at the Forth Bridge and the first bomb in Edinburgh fell at the end of Kinnear Road in Inverleith, the crater of which provided a lot of interest. Leith was, I think, the only area in Edinburgh to sustain serious damage. The longest alert we had was on the night of the Clydeside bombings. We were huddled in the bathroom which Bones reckoned to be the safest part of the house. I dozed in the bath for the duration of that night.

I remember feeling some alarm when Bones would slip to the front room to view the searchlights and the enemy planes. The air-raid shelters provided in the back-greens were damp and musty and seldom, if ever, used. Joan joined the ATS (the women's army) when she was seventeen and a half, and after training at Dalkeith, she was posted to south Wales. By means of cross-postings she worked her way back to Edinburgh and was engaged in John Watson's School, then taken over by the army. Alan had to join the Home Guard at College, and would spend weekends reluctantly crawling about the King's Park on manoeuvres with his face blackened with burnt cork. Firewatching afforded a good source of income for students, with the going rate at ten shillings a night, and for some, it constituted their permanent digs, local students standing in during vacations. For some time Alan did regular firewatching at the billiards saloon in Leith Street—and got plenty of free games. VE Day brought the release of all the pent-up tensions and was celebrated to the full. There were singing and dancing in the streets and Princes Street was athrong with people of all ages. The American forces were on the balcony of their club in Princes Street, now the Mount Royal Hotel, singing and throwing gum to the crowds below.

When Alan started at the Veterinary College in 1942 he had to obtain some horses' bones to study. As he couldn't afford to buy these, he went off to the knackery at Saughton to get his own specimens, and returned with two smelly sacks containing a skull, hooves, some vertebrae and some long bones, which had not been too well cleaned. Nonplussed, Mum set about the grisly task. As with stock for broth, she boiled them all until they were clean. They were then put up on the roof to be purified by the sun. It is difficult to describe the smell that hung about the house for some considerable time. To some young visitors we became known as 'the house with the piano and the horse in the box'.

Joan and I had been sent to piano lessons but we made little of it. The natural musical flair was vested solely in Alan who learned the clarinet and the saxophone and was self-taught for jazz and swing on the piano. He became a regular in the Dick Vet dance band. Perhaps it was because of Alan's activities that my teenage years seem to have been dominated by the music of the time, which, unlike the pop music of the '60s, '70s and '80s, seems to be more enduring—or is this the fantasy of age? The great names then were—Glenn Millar, Nat King Cole, Duke Ellington, Louis Armstrong, Benny Goodman, Harry James, Bunny Berrigan, Stan Kenton, the two Dorseys, Hoagy Carmichael, Ted Heath, Fats Waller, Count Basie, Joe Loss, Nellie Lutcher, etc—with music like—'Sunny Side of the Street', 'In the Mood', 'Take the A Train', 'Laura', 'Sky Liner', 'Hey, Babareebab', 'Girl in Calico', '12th Street Rag', 'Scatterbrain', 'Stardust', 'Elmer's Tune', 'Honeysuckle Rose', 'The Way You Look To-night', 'A Huggin and A Chalkin', 'Big Noise Blew in from Winnetca', and so on. We crouched round the HMV radiogram to hear Alan's collection of records of these stalwarts. It was, therefore, a major catastrophe when they were accidentally knocked off the narrow bookshelf where he stored them. These were the days of the thriving dance halls, the main ones in Edinburgh being the Plaza, New Cavendish and Palais de Danse, where the vogue was quicksteps, slow foxtrots, sambas, tangos, waltzes and the jitterbug. I was never one for dancing despite efforts to teach me by Alan and Joan, but I enjoyed watching them swapping the latest twists, turns and manoeuvres that they had picked up.

Music is one of the things that seems to afford a link with people; such associations in the family are:

Kielder Grandpa—'Rose of Tralee'
Auntie Nettie—'Juanita'
Auntie Nan—'Deep in the Wood' and the Glasgow Orpheus Choir
Auntie Lizzie—'Any Old Iron'
Uncle John—'I'll Walk Beside You'
Mum—'Smilin' Through' or, in lighter mood, 'Have You Ever Seen a Dream Walking?'
Bones—John McCormick's 'Star of the County Down'
Cathie—'Any Umbrellas'

Mum used to say that if she was ever reincarnated, she would wish to be a singer.

The late 1940s saw the first permanent split in the family unit, when Alan graduated and found a job in a veterinary practice in Great Yarmouth. There he met and married June and a new family unit was born. Joan, by then demobilised from the Forces, followed suit a few years later with David, and I—

well—I plodded on to become a faceless Civil Servant, spending my spare time active at tennis, badminton, golf etc, at least until I jouked my back.

Bones retired in 1961 after over forty-five years on the railways, earning a handsome gold watch and a pension of eleven shillings a week! He took on odd jobs to occupy his new-found leisure—summer work as a warder at Holyrood set him off learning some of the finer details of Scottish history, and his natural skills at parcel tying were appreciated as the odd-job man in Boswall's travel goods shop in Hanover Street. He died in 1970 after a coronary attack.

Alan, Joan and I were with Mum when she died very peacefully on 5 December 1987.

She had been at Gairloch on her last holiday in 1986. She was always happiest at the sea.

Glossary of Terms

Bagatelle:	game played on a board with nine balls and a fixed spring cue, the object being to put the balls into numbered areas.
Chiffonier:	an ornamental cupboard.
Crash Pinny:	coarse strong linen pinafore.
Deal table:	pine table.
Diabolo:	game with two-headed top spun on a string slung between two sticks.
French cricket:	simplified form of cricket, using legs as stumps.
Goffering irons:	tool used to crimp ruffles.
Gowans:	wild marguerites.
Guiders:	home-made cart steered by a rope.
Huck napkin:	linen napkin.
Jouk:	wrench.
Kist:	chest.
Latching a rug:	making a rag rug; the latches are the loops of material.
Leevoy:	a type of hide and seek.
Mutch:	linen cap.
Parsing:	telling the parts of speech of a

	sentence and the relations of the various words to each other.
Partans:	large crabs.
Peeries:	spinning tops.
Peevers:	hopscotch.
Pin:	as much washing as will go through a mangle at one time.
Plum duff:	plum pudding.
Poke:	paper bag.
Press:	cupboard.
Rubbers:	rubber-soled canvas shoes.
Running messages:	getting the shopping.
Siver:	drain.
Statues:	game involving freezing like a statue.
Stone pigs:	earthenware hot water bottles.
Tinnies:	small tin mugs.
Vackies:	evacuees.
Velour:	velvet.
Wilks:	whelks.